The Chalk Butterfly

Jane Monson

Cinnamon Press
:: small miracles from distinctive voices ::

Published by Cinnamon Press
www.cinnamonpress.com
The right of Jane Monson to be identified as author of this work has been
asserted by her in accordance with the Copyright, Designs and Patent Act,
1988. © 2022, Jane Monson
ISBN 978-1-78864-129-6
British Library Cataloguing in Publication Data. A CIP record for this
book can be obtained from the British Library.
Designed and typeset in Bodoni by Cinnamon Press. Cover design by
Adam Craig © Adam Craig.
Cinnamon Press is represented by Inpress

Acknowledgements

Some of *The Chalk Butterfly* has been previously published and I would
like to thank the following editors for their print and online acceptance of
the following:

'Sylvie's River' in *What Lies Within* (Liquorice Fish, 2017). 'Taming the
Sand,' 'Was Home,' 'Confiscated Wings,' 'Road Art' (renamed 'The Chalk
Butterfly'), in *The Fortnightly Review*: https://fortnightlyreview.co.uk/
2020/09/prose-poems/. 'The Secret Life of Mud' in *The Westerly*, 63.1
(2018) and 'The Patchwork Boy' in 63. 2 (November, 2018). 'The
Undersound,' in 'Six Poets; Many Voices': Disability Feature, *Westerly
Magazine*: https://westerlymag.com.au/issues/westerly-disability/. 'The
Wall and the Butterfly,' 'The Secret Life of Mud,' 'The Girl and the
Octopus,' 'Taming the Sand,' 'The Shared Plot' and 'Road Art,' in *The
Beltway Poetry Quarterly* (August 2021): www.beltwaypoetry.com). 'The
Blind Window' and 'The Chalk Butterfly' in *Alcatraz* (forthcoming, 2022).
'The Story of Ice and Us,' 'Haunted Objects,' 'Method' and the 'Book in
the Mountain,' in Axon: Creative Explorations Journal: (https://
www.axonjournal.com.au/issues), 2021. 'The Girl and the Octopus,' was
shortlisted in the *Aesthetica* Creative Writing Competition (2020) and
published in the competition's anthology. Thanks to Jon O'Connor and all
at The School Bus Project, for audio recordings of 'Roadsong' and 'The
Wall and the Butterfly' as part of the project's 5th birthday celebrations:
https://www.schoolbusproject.org/sbp5-2015-2020. To the brilliant online
poetry series, Litbalm, for the 'Rooms and Spaces' reading with Holly
Iglesias, Rodger Kamenetz and Paul Hetherington, curated by
Cassandra Atherton and hosted by Marc Vincenz and Jonathan Penton:
https://www.youtube.com/watch?v=siLWQMhp3qQ.

Heartfelt gratitude to Jan Fortune, Adam Craig and all at Cinnamon Press and Liquorice Fish for their care, passion and commitment to my work and prose poetry in general. Huge appreciation to all the poets who took the time and care to review and blurb the book as well as help me re-appreciate the poems in other ways. To friends and family (especially Jon and Mandy O'Connor, Hugo Azérad, Jane de Lozey, Sheelagh Neuling and Cat Paterson) for all the conversations, opportunities to share poems and your consistent encouragement. I would also like to thank the immeasurable guidance—editorial and otherwise—of the brilliant Kaddy Benyon (individually and as part of the Sidney Poetry group—Lucy Sheerman, Lucy Hamilton, Stav Poleg and the late Clare Crossman), without whom this book would still be meandering, scattered and stalling. To Niki Sotudeh, Kaddy Benyon, Stav Poleg, Cassandra Atherton (fellow Fairy-godmother of prose poetry), Ben Walker, Patricia Debney, Rosie O'Connor, Lindsay Fursland and Joanna Rachel for their engaged, significant read-throughs, time and invaluable critiques. To Cassandra always, Eileen Fursland and Lilleith Morrison for their unwavering love, support and passion for my creative and critical work. To the London writing group and the next collection you're inspiring. To Kiran, whose kindness and clear guidance through every challenge, ensured I could stay on course. Likewise, the NHS, CFS support and AEDS—a small way of saying I can't thank you enough. Finally, to my world of Niki and Sylvie —for being who you are and where you are, always—I couldn't do it without you.

Contents

Stage Four: Egg Overwintered

The Soul has Bandaged Moments

Emily Dickinson

To home and its unseen inhabitants
—dying, living, changing, unfathomable—

The Chalk Butterfly

Stage One: The Patient Wing

.

The Undersound

There is a place from which she intends to move. Where her listless breath on the glass has made a stranger of the view outside, the movement of people beyond the gate pure murmur. She doesn't watch paint dry, she hears it. There goes the cheap white gloss stretch and snap off the sill and skirting, the rust chafes on the gate's hinge, working in shrill intervals through the letter box. And across it all the white noise of indoored-words: ceiling, curtain, carpet, tap. One day, dressed in her finest stage regalia, she assured them outside that she was fine—they could sign her off on the promise of a mood diary, repeat prescriptions, reviews. She soon ran out of journals, found herself approaching the walls. Began scratching at their decorated layers when her voice failed, peeling her paper throat down to the floor, marking in red the daily targets that began to sleep in the corridors. Now each room is a graphic novel of her as past, present and potential—she reels them out at random, switching the order of the rooms and stories, choosing her own adventure. Sometimes she hears the sea as through a shell. Sometimes it's the tinnitus, growing inside and under her from the absence of doorbells, of wind through willows, a bird hatching, planes blooming near the roof, cars screeching through red lights. She hears the sounds without the instruments. Drowns in them first, from where they come, later.

The Wrong Blossom

In April, she opens the window to snow. Not falling, but banked up from floor to roof, pressed and packed as a prisoner's wall. More features than brick, but just as unwelcoming.

The Wall and the Butterfly

He closes his mouth ahead of the butterflies; holds his tongue before they take flight. Hand over eyes, he protects himself from the air's impossible movements; stills his head mid-swarm. They've been told to build the wall here anyway; to ensure each and every hand that reaches for a tool, a machine, keeps going in spite of their native wings. But their skin is his story too. His touch, their fall. He watches the way his flesh changes under the hurricane of the butterfly swarm, tattooed by pollen and the colours of wing-dust and burnt journeys. In under a hammer blow, the sky clouds from insect to bird. Scissor-tailed Flycatchers, Olive Sparrows, Green Jays, and Clay-coloured Thrushes pile about the working frames, dry-drown them in pounding flutters. A tree of Great-tailed Grackles explodes in applause. Over the troubled soil, Zebra Heliconians, Giant Orange Sulphurs, Monarchs, Queens, Soldiers and Red-bordered Pixies flicker at their marching feet. Unable to move, he opens his mouth and loses his tongue. To every brick, gun and metal force, they raise their wings; state their place in the chain of us: what we eat, what we are and what we could be inside the colours of open hands.

The Undone

Fading inside her is the memory of a man she had known for a long time. At least twenty years she'd calculated, straight after he came home to tell her the way he'd voted. The same hand that registered their vows on one piece of paper undid them by a cross on another. She couldn't take in what needed to follow, so focussed on place, things and furniture; not just her own, but theirs—the other men to blame that had also split houses; heaved the lives of their family into something they didn't choose, didn't sign up to. Emptying her life of rooms she'd made with him, she leans her back against another temporary wall. Watches paper blister on the one opposite and in her new imagination conjures into the room his shadow. It sits behind America's most legendary desk and orders the room back to 'sunburst'. It replaces busts, rugs, curtains—anything of colour, except gold. She replays a nightmare of him carefully choosing the next pen; smirking over the replacement of his predecessor's hand as he forces its unfamiliar shape into the snub of his fingers. She sees his face loom into focus as the crowd is blurred out. A vacant sweep across each document, he waves the golden pen, aims then fires— commits his name to the undoing of nature, earth, countries, states, skin, families, children, hope; casts their futures back into their pasts; cast hers back into a past that until recently, promised to exist as a future.

The Secret Life of Mud

Eyes to the ground, backs to the sky, in London a new rise of
searchers. Their eyes-only approach less the keen, blunting nose
of a machine than a slow scour of land; an English Waltz of reach,
pick-up and burrow in the short-term dark of a working pocket.
Meet the Mudlarks, roaming and combing the foreshore in the
quiet margin of the river's grave. They are the new Bone
Grubbers, the Scavengers, Sewer Hunters by choice. With
permits and skills they re-home the stuff of chance; retell the
stone's flight, the story of metal, cloth or leather caught in some
bend of wind and planted along the water road. Once found and
recorded, objects of note are cleaned and re-settled behind glass
in the mapped-out belly of a museum. The clay pipes, toy stone
men on horses, mint-faced coins from a million hands ago, boots
whose tread and crease have stepped through 500 years and
spoons from the mouths of every age, are given the chance to
speak again. And this is what we might hear them say: *thanks to
the mud we lived in the dark and thanks to the air, we'll die in the
light.*

Little Theatres

A brief chaos of hair across her forehead, sardonically tamed over a carefully made-up eye. The girl on her lap sticks out a tongue as far as the tip of her chin, while the eye under the wayward fringe glowers from a tipped-back head. Each girl bares her teeth wide in the reflection. They've chosen the faded orange pleated curtain as their background this time. Hospital-blue does their skin no favours. All eyes on show are bubbling with laughter, brows reaching up towards the hairline. Earrings become scraps of light in the bulb's flash, and tightly choreographed curls styled this morning are carelessly undone, tatty from an unscripted wind and a rush into the city. These little theatres serve them well; quick dive off the street into a micro-chamber, curtains drawn, coins shoved in, cue sound and visuals; eyes braced for the bright pop of the camera. Their untitled love started when they were learning to sit up and eat. Now exam-eyed and party-tired, they slip whenever they can into windowless spaces; outdoor rooms of their own, after school, on the weekends, during the long holidays. Squashed and giggling they create noise while they can; take in themselves and exhale as much of the world's spoiled air as humanly possible, while the small spinning chair reels clock-wise and anti-clockwise beneath them. Outside, their blithe freedom slides down a small chute, waits un-repeated in a passport strip and shivers in a machine-led wind that fixes it dry.

18

Revolving Stage

The first thing they do when they walk through the sliding door is rub their hands. They are not pleased with themselves, nor ready for action; neither are they coming in from the cold. They've been directed by a man behind a speaker to sanitize themselves before entering. In various states of shock, they're liable to trip onto the stage and forget. Once on the other side, they wait, sometimes forever before being taken into electric white rooms divided into smaller rooms, made of swaying or hurriedly closed Pantone blue curtains, 300 on the colour chart for the medical shade. The evening is fractured into several noises, some disembodied, others shouting in front of them before vanishing and lessening in the corridors. Over the sight of blood and frantically wrapped home-bound bandages, the last thing they hear is the silence of a sleeping girl, wheeled through in her sparkling dress and long auburn curls, hanging down the side of her new chair, moving without care past her arm, not quite finished with dancing.

Guiding

On the bus, a woman in a coat that pours over the floor is talking to a stranger through her guide dog. *Aren't you gorgeous and how do you keep yourself so clean? Look at the colour of your fur!* The stranger seated opposite replies, bending her head towards her companion that yes, her coat is darker in the winter, that she grooms herself most of the time. The bus switches from side roads onto the main stretch towards the hospital. Here the sun is low— in and out of the driver's eyes, the city all over the passenger windows; its film of old rain, gum and hand-drawn curses, filtering the afternoon's rays. At the front where the two women sit, the light becomes more interrogating. The bus pulls into the hospital as the owner and her dog start to rise. Heavily seated, but light of tongue, the woman leans over the puddle of her coat, raises her head and declares that *the sun is so bright, it almost blinds you.* They continue to stand with a brief pause over the woman's face. As they leave, she thanks the driver and makes her way towards the main entrance, smiling and showing the world the well-rehearsed spark of her laughter.

The Slow Sail Home

The old woman's smile is inside-out, skew-whiff. The girl is pale, youngish, refusing tea, watching the woman's words lean over the sides of her mouth. She follows her dutifully around the house, around the questions, circling for answers. The old woman turns to her, a sway in her eyes in which the girl loses balance. They shift and tilt like this for a while, and by the time the sun is over the yard-arm, the wind peters out, leaves her sails empty. Her body rebalances, evens out under a clear blue sky. The girl begins to recognise her grandmother as before, the way her mouth dances with her eyes, the way the child in her peers out; the way her expression can fall like leaves shocked by an oddly timed cold snap and her smile like a flood of sun through the branches. Then the old woman yawns and tells the girl to go, not because she's bored, but she's noticed her coat is still on and that she's refused tea at least twice.

The Mime Garden

Under the stroke of my grandmother's hand, the wall has cultivated a shadow where a handrail should be. Outside, she says is trouble; inside she can't get broken, so long as she sticks to the blooming shadows she's made at home. Each time I visit, she gets me to deadhead the roses in the wallpaper.

Blue Vodka Dress

The story you told about stepping from a tram in Russia and the air being so strong you could have lit it with a match, made us laugh. Elbows on your knees, palms holding the weight of your chin, crooked fingers like vines across your walled cheeks, you watched our faces twitch with all the unease and hysteria you had hoped for.

The story yesterday was different. From the point of view of a girl you'd known since she was an hour old, walking into your room to find your brittle-boned arm buried in a drawer of socks, fishing for the morning Smirnoff, the beginning of which was hiding in the apple juice behind your typewriter. On top of the cup, a carefully balanced plate of cherries, each one a reward for a single clattered-out sentence.

By sundown, a time-jumbled opening to a novel about a mum of five moving between countries, West, East, then West again—torn between the blossoming corals of the Red Sea and green canopied trails of the Vienna Woods. Beneath the fruit, was the story you wanted to tell.

When you were fully witnessed, the room lost control and the scolded girl was ordered to put all the objects back, without touching the paper or the typewriter. Not so much the fall, than the plate, the sly cup, the clear glass bottle which you'd assembled for the day, that changed her memories of you, your blue vodka dress and the way you moved inside it. More liquid than cloth, it fell about you like a bad joke; the stitches and flowers placed with cruel regularity under the downward slew of cherry pips.

Stage Two: Chrysalis, Not Cocoon

The Weathering

Mist has set-in, boat-wrecks already in the making as the sky and sea slip quietly inside each other. A cloud for a brain, fog for thought—a sheep-shaped indecision—parks and settles into the snug of her skull. She has things coming up: deadlines. Tries holding a book open: can see the words, knows all the letters, their tails, curves, bridges and towers, but the dial between their sense is halfway between stations. She's been told to submit, not to fight. So, she abandons the task, the list, the aim; sits out the cold on the vague side of meaning; settles for the view outside— raises her eyes to a window. This is what she sees when blind-ish. A fuzz of trees, triangles of slanting roofs, some slate, others clay, patches of bleached moss, bird drops, rectangular and square white frames around windows, the odd human crowding against the glass. Sky the shade of sea. Flickers of birds scrawled against the grey. A black V here, then m, then W. But they're not frequent enough to hold her and she finds herself willing a murmur or two, just to say she's done something today. Read the sky at least.

Haunted Objects

Whenever he placed a hand on a wall, bench or building, he heard things; imprints of the last bit of their story. Inside the sounds—palm pressed flat into the stone, metal or wood—he also saw things; witnessed unseen the last drawn scrap of their view. Tracks, alleys, roads, rooms, screams, glass, falls, arms drowning in black, poker-red and ashen air. With each life, he felt too much and was blown backwards across space, hurt and bewildered. Recovery wasn't possible without touch and he was offered gloves every other time he was found with his hands open, crying someone else's tears.

Growing a Thought in Snow

The sky is set to flake and peel. Unadorned elms and silver
birches lean a little further towards the ground in memory of
wood. The more cloud-borne arms split into stick figures, brittle
and unwilling to puncture the bloated air. Some talk in shivering
groups beneath the inconceivable weight of clouds. Others stretch
their arms and try to steady themselves; a childlike jumble of
tipping points. A few wait patiently for new limbs; stand like
pillars until then, arms hibernating inside their trunks, until a
protruding knot for a shoulder, elbow and wrist where a hand
could be. Nubs and nodules, the gradual shoot of spikes; how
each year they come too late or in the wrong order. Snow in
summer, blossom in winter, ash in spring, the limbs far from ready
for petals before the freeze, the blaze; snow and fire falling from
their reach like a child's first catch. The fractalled white collects
inside the spaces and when it settles, we are left with a stick-child
creaking, its half-formed cradle choking on the air, spindly arms
crying from the strain of sky.

Dance of the Blind Ballerina

They give themselves away through breath—a light cough from the girl with the bandaged eyes, a choked snigger from the blind ballerina. When they speak their voices are about the same age. The girl with the cloth eyes does not ask for the other girl's name, but wants to know what she loves, who she wants to be and where. She tells her she dances, that she's a ballerina and although she doesn't want to be here, she doesn't know where yet. One eye-watering beat, they drop, play dead—hear the wind take the remains of an unhinged door. As the light breaks, walls explode and stone thunders over them; glass bursts like a failed dam out of houses and cars and their bodies lie scrunched up within a shoe of each other. The dancer remains silent, then during the interval, urges her feet and hands awake—fans out, spins into the air; pirouettes the nameless space around them. The girl feels dizzy; she knows the dark, but not when it's stirred. Her nylon eyes itch, her stomach shivers—she can taste the dust spun up from the floor and tries to smell where they are. Throwing out her arms, she unleashes them into the air and grabs random pockets of heat from the ballerina. She tastes ash, the wind's acrid breath, feels where the dust is at its thickest—remembers falling upwards, landing with smoke, grit, rubble. They do not touch; miss each other by a whisper.

Icarus

Your back was land seen from a plane, American land of scorched soil and rock: Idaho, Utah, East Oregon; the red, cratered earth that fell too close to the sun. On your back, over the shoulder blade, you were land divided: the skin, a careful place riddled with mines and keep out signs.

The Patchwork Boy

This is the story of a boy who was burnt and put together by the skin of his hometown. His mother was first in line, giving the best of an unsteady arm to be grafted onto her first born, while his father followed, offering whatever was needed from wherever was useful or young enough. The word got out and bit by bit the boy became something of himself again. He had never given much thought to skin, unless knocked or cut, but now he couldn't get away from the stuff. He was told about it in all sorts of ways. It was an amount, an adoption, a journey—150 pieces from a man here, 200 from a woman there; a subtracting of stories pinhead by pinhead. He wondered if they would feel less of who they were while he began to look more of who he was, before his pockets lit up. The papers described the process as an upholstering—he was the patchwork, the swatch, the continuity boy. It didn't go unnoticed that his undoing began their doing; took his burnt flesh to become the fabric of the community. He saw things otherwise; he was the boy who couldn't come to the town, so the town came to him. They crossed themselves through his door, darkened his windows and scratched their charity into his walls; bar chart by bar chart the Dr tracked the donations. Beside his head, thousands of shut black gates, doll-dimensioned fences. In front of him, the open and shut window; a twitching eye that framed the place where he ended and they began.

Roadsong

Climbing the hill to Assisi the bus shuddered up the corkscrew path of the mountain. Walls of white rock crumbled under the sun, the earth dropped far below to the left, then right. Villages, horses and carts, fruit trees and believers, blurred and mixed in a haze, miles beneath the sight-seers' feet. A blind man, whose skin mapped out every Umbrian road this side of Perugia, sang to himself; distracted the passengers from the dust muting their shocked reflections as the wheels nudged the cliff-edges. The song knew the roads well, unwavering at the turns, sailing the route to the church at the top, taking them carefully through every line that moved about his face. On the last bend, before the view coaxed gasps from the crowd, the man stopped singing and a young girl opposite saw his face deepening into crevices, splintering around his eyes and mouth, like land cracking impossibly fast into drought.

The Lesson in Smell

Before the class begins, the table is set: herbs, spices and powdered petals gathered in the pinch of her fingers and moved into small glass caves with punctuated ceilings. Unlabelled, each pot is passed around reluctant hands. They lift each scent to their nose—a flinch, a near-smile and a screwed-up forehead animate the thawing landscapes of their skin. Zig-zagging between time and place, a woman worries inside her chair; lowers her face over the memory triggers and breathes her way across history. The road I see by cinnamon, she says, leads to her grandfather and the only daughter he had, then ignored; a secret by the name of Amandine, whose body free-falling the buildings of Paris, screamed silently past a typically smiling head of a woman, crowning the lintel of an open window. Next bottle, a man says distantly, is more taste than smell: tiramisu—the last thing he had in a restaurant. She watches his eyes close to the layers of song in cream, coffee and cocoa dust. Then the oldest voice in the room, hovering between Farsi and English—*Nārenji? Orange?*—unsure of where to land in fruit or colour. At the far end of the table is a young girl, who dutifully sniffs each pot that comes and goes through her hands, but watched by the ring of adults, fires out 'toast!' and whispers, 'don't know this one.' The pictures will come once they stop looking. Smell for her, still a very recent journey.

The Girl and the Octopus

This is the story of the match girl and the dreaming octopus; where they meet, but do not speak and where they part, but do not leave. A place where a tentacle finds its way around a hand. Where the pictures that appear from a match-struck wall by a barefoot girl in snow, twin the cinematic gleam and fade inside a sleeping mollusc. The deep sea holds its night breath and fixes around the light-changing phenomena, while the girl's visions begin away from her: each lit match throws out a moving picture the length of a tiny wooden stalk. The cephalopod sleeps on, and we see her dream in flecked shades of gold, white, lavender and black; blooming patterns illuminate, then fade accordingly. In one scene a tentacle undoes like a time-lapsed fern, stretching away from her third heart; in another she is the seafloor, all coral, sand and dancing kelp. Far inland, to the bright orange bomb of each flicker, brick walls around houses dissipate and the girl stirs to a crackling hearth, a New Year's table, carefully laid with crystal, pearl and silver. Another strike brings plum-stuffed goose with apple and a Christmas tree; children reflected in glass ornaments, their faces rosy under the candle-lights. Finally, her grandmother, smiling beside her bed again. Undoing the mollusc's grip from her sleeping fingers, the old woman lifts the girl, balloon-light towards the stars; where they meet, but do not speak, where they touch and do not leave.

Method

The air does not separate us; we do not separate in the air. It takes from our skin, hair, blood, waste, words, sweat, tears and laughter, cooks us in the wind and bakes the whole damn earth together. At least that's what the recipe says. The one we never follow.

The Bruised Rose

On her skin, parts of the city left small islands of colour she recognised from plums, bark after the rain, walls behind smoke, night sea under mist and lighting used to soften bars. She remembered phases of the night; young expressions losing definition in the cross-fire of cigarettes and perpetual rounds. Moving in herds from place to place—she recalled sections of walls, furniture, doors, full then empty streets—their voices, then hers, un-meeting. Remembered a shelter, then her reflection in the bus window; amber streetlights breaking like yolk over the shaking pictures as the driver moved recklessly through the centre towards the suburbs. The discipline it took to stand up and press the bell, greasy metal in her hands as she held onto the pole while the bus slowed, swung around a corner, bumped her down the step into the streets and on toward a version of home. She felt the city close its eyes around her, throw rain in her face, tease her feet around moving street-signs and landmarks, heave its roots through cracks in the paving slabs. Mostly the bruises flowered with memory over her limbs, but there was one she couldn't read. So, she waited, watched; taut as a cat, just before something in the wind sets its pounce alight.

The Glass Kiss

Our mother was the unhinged child on the floor of a supermarket. When it came to orders from Doctors she thrashed her legs, kept her fingers rigid as bookends against her ears, scrunched up her eyes and screamed in defiance. Deep into adulthood, the epilepsy roiled inside her while she drank down the pills and fell at parties, rode a bicycle in worn-out sandals—no helmet, throwing the bike against all weathers. Inside the house no better, putting guards around the gas fires long after the scars had forced the story of her tameless skin. Once, maybe twice, she took us to the cinema, where we learnt to understand it wasn't the pictures, nor the film noir embraces and promises, the Chaplinesque misdemeanours and crescendo in the music, but the lights; the flickering switches between scenes, that made her eyes fix wide and disappear, her hands swell and hammer on the row in front. We remember her voice sowing echoes into the dark, the silhouettes of people fleeing and the sound of flip seats thudding out of rhythm. Laurel and Hardy pushing a piano on repeat up a flight of stairs, then vanishing before time as the houselights came up.

Was Home

Last night a moth confused his throat for cloth, fraying the words each time he tried to let them out. The best part of his life was spent creating and finishing sound, watertight sentences. Now he faces her daily at a funny angle: cranes headlong into the past to see how he might have arrived at memory or meaning. The house is starting to record the home's absence; plays it back to them at bedtime. In the floor's creaks and groans they relive all the battles and defeats; the refrain of each other's roars and whimpers. The radio keeps a grip on time every other day, unevenly sharing their space like a disembodied lodger, the mouth that never needs feeding. They move in and out of its rotating clatter and calm while the paper keeps coming away from the walls and the chairs look vaguely at the table. One of these days, someone might witness them through the window. Get what it's like to have the person you know more than you know yourself move out of light into shadow.

The Kindness of Windows

The light shifts and trips sideways; unlearns its stance against the walls and creates a mockery of shadows. The window opens kindly and the night leaps out, followed by moths, hungry from another empty harvest.

Stage Three: The Hungry Skin

The Porous Border

Lately, much of the world has got under her skin. Between waking and sleeping, her face is lit screen after screen: small frame, big frame, small frame in that order daily. Make that: much of the world gets onto her skin; inside it; instead of it.

Taming the Sand

The desert blows in at the door and rises to the table where the meal is set; reshapes itself around the room and fades each object to a grit-charged mist. Trees that stood sentry across the dunes are vanishing too; their scorched backs once resilient to the sun, curl comma-like, bowing closer to the earth through the year. The villagers construct low square walls of straw into the sand. They plan to grow these walls like seeds—repeat them without pardon over the land into a giant net—square straw fractals to capture a pillaging storm; to measure the pattern of its outlawed dust and hold its stone fibres to account. Witnesses recall the way it wrecked the vines that grew the grapes that fell to raisins and kept the families; illustrate for the jury how it covers dark field beds in yellow like an infertile pollen that insists upon the land, breath by breath. How their exposed skin does what the fruit should— burns, shrinks into itself, dries out to a last gift. They protest from a desiccated sea, the tide less flow, more ebb with each season they fail to hold in their arms and harvest. The unwelcome wind awaits the verdict as their voices begin to disappear. Time pours out through itself and the jury is left weighing up what they heard and what they saw: something about a land they could once predict chasing its own ending.

The English Lesson

A wind not felt anywhere—on record—quite like this, threw down into the roots of an English Oak, lifted all 200 years of her and slammed her back to earth. Rerouting herself over years back into the ground, she taught the other trees something they'd have to remember at the next unknown blast from this warped haven, this anti-biosphere: keep drawing up what they can't see, haven't yet touched, tasted nor understood.

The Book in the Mountain

Upon hearing that in geological terms, the scientists were trying to read the sedimentary layers in the rocks of Italy to determine whether or not an asteroid had hit the earth and changed the course of the dinosaurs, she turned to me and said: *they're trying to find the words in the mountain*. Layers like pages of a book, the land all pressed into itself like a sleeping accordion. And the words they were trying to find were fossils; insect and leaf tightly bound inside the traumatised soil.

The Story of Ice and Us

From Glacier to dead ice, her remains after the summer-melt, slump and rise with the sea-line. In her place, a plaque, a memorial for Okjökull: Ode to a Glacier. Janus-faced it stands in stone and shadow as Elegy and Omen: *we know what is happening and what needs to be done.* She dies a living mantle of dogged ice, moving under the weight of herself defined by name and skin; a frozen garment of stories, *histories of the atmosphere,* laid waste at our all-knowing hands. We provide a threadbare coat over the puddle—into which tread bears, under which flee fish. Against the wind they cross borders; through the lines where we wait and harvest fear from our towns and houses. Land and sea are each other's worries now and living things can't settle between them. Wildfires of earth and ocean; field and Arctic's topsoil alike, rewritten as a charcoal sea. Inside these worlds of ink and paper, type and screen, we absorb, reflect, and try and bounce the light back into space. Glacier, dead ice, bloating waters, we read on: listen to some characters, skip others, laugh in disbelief, cry at bears haunting bin-lined streets and toppled gates. Mostly, we sit comfortably, stay awake at the good bits, read by the blindness of fires, until shut-eyed we let the whole thing melt away in and from our hands.

The Shared Plot

A dove grey bird flies between the air pockets of a small tree. Other than its flight, no discernible wind. It is the last tree for miles, stalled by the edge of a road that leads the odd foot and wheel into a village. Host to a bird whose song was chased towards the ground, whose winged phrase has always sung down upon a branch, the tree has slowly quietened. A bird and tree whose native sounds, names and habits have been clear-felled; from language, from care, from here—whose lessening measures our story and the ways we refuse to live.

Split-Screened Earth

Bone-carved, dust-dried legs from the knee down, resting on threadbare sandals atop a threadbare earth, she is captured, framed, sold, unseen. Her earth is fragmented, in pieces like ill-preserved paper or an unglazed biscuit finish. There is a hint of wet in one corner of the photograph as if we need the drought defined. Her feet work the land without causing a single, hairline crack. On the opposite page of the centrefold, a boy takes off his shoes and socks and the waxy palms of his feet disappear in the carpet pile. In the mansion's hallway, a girl skates as fast as possible across a parquet floor, her hands over her eyes and mouth agape as she glosses over her reflection.

The Chalk Butterfly

She'd landed face down on a chalk drawing of a butterfly. Beside her the bicycle wheels span, hummed through her last impression of the world. The street was otherwise quiet and there were no known witnesses. In their absence, nature stepped up. Jackdaws at the crossroad spoke for everyone: each turn is tight, cramped and nobody wants to give way or slow down. A tree—one of the tallest in the area, all vertical branches and feathering leaves—agreed; through every wise listening leaf, agreed. Reticent at first, objects pitched in. The old red pillar box—diagonally across from her body—stood reliably gaping in a dignified manner and announced that its chipped iron aperture would soon receive letters and sympathy cards. The road sighed under a sharp gust; a stone, edged from the kerb onto the middle bar of a drain, clanged, then dropped into a tiny wet echo. A bird or more would have been startled, flown in any direction and only resettled after the sirens. Cats, dogs, squirrels, may twitch every so often in recollection. Insects darting to unusual vibrations, perished or were injured in the process. Today with no threat of rain there remains just a chalk butterfly; its dust ever so slightly smudged at the left wing, where she'd kissed it with everything she had in her at the time.

Hand to Mouth

Red, sun-lit and slurring across the pavement from the shop door towards the gutter, the blood becomes a tributary—and a decision—among pedestrians. The ritual of dense shuffling and bumping shoulders, stops as they question their next step. Warned by a nervous cluster looking down to witness the city's sly river gleaming inches from their feet, a portion of the morning's rush hour starts to slow and quieten. Some raise a hand to mouth or cross themselves, others mutter *God* into a nearby shoulder and a young face curdles with age. A woman freezes, grips her fingers around her bag before one shoe rises, suspends then retracts in the air, turning back towards the shops. Behind her they've started closing, banging down their metal shutters, slamming their doors and fumbling their signs around. Both feet panic and the road she runs into is blocked and choking with cars. Unwittingly, others follow her, fighting and hurling themselves between metal-encased strangers, shouting the odds through their horns. On the other side of the street, a few stand their ground and watch from a distance at the chaos of hands and stooped backs, bent towards a head and stomach wrapped and knotted in cloth, torn from a person's back. One shirt is finished, before another is needed and people start undressing, binding the young man like children attend the wounded in a living-room play. The folds over the head start to dry, but his heart keeps giving until the cloth stops moving. From outside the crowd a wail, all too thin, high and late. The eyes of the drivers close for a minute, turn their keys in unison and the engines start warming, wheels rolling forward as red turns to green, then blue.

This Side of Things

Black and split as a shed raven's feather, her hair breaks against the coastline of her profile as she speaks about the state of things. Her features become the rocks that define the shape of the land, the mouth a soft border depending on who crosses it. It looks unused these days: an old port, an empty depot. The view this side of her face is of the land crumbling; limits where people have come and gone, trodden the same ground in hope. But lately the heart's been dug up, slung out to sea where even the fish let it pass. And that hair—like an old pair of drapes limp and faded— is grateful for as much as a cough or a sneeze. She says it's the earth, not her voice that's the problem. That her voice always worked with the world, but now the earth is winded, cornered, awkward; nothing like we would want to find it.

At the Listener's Edge

Mind is a state as much as a gap, she preached at her friend, who in a state, was measuring her life in gaps that the mind couldn't fill. Mark your words, the friend thought: the biggest gap you can't see is between my mind and me.

Milk Tooth

When she felt the fizzing in her hands, she picked up her pocket radio, turned it up so the family couldn't hear what was coming. But they noticed the frequency and would race to her through the noise under the random music and news bulletins. Her body electric, they'd find her on the floor, the bed, under a table—a woman subsumed by bad signals and an ill-fated dialogue between body and brain. She cycles, marches for peace, equal rights and fights daily for money, a home. This is not her sofa, this is not her bed, this is not her house. And neither is the next one, nor the next. As children, this might have been fun, but the mother is not translating the light side well; not showing them that this is an adventure, rather than a world they need to navigate without wings. The girl remembers a house where her milk teeth began falling, one tooth in particular where she took the advice of a cartoon, got a piece of a string, hammocked it between her mouth and a door handle and told her brother to slam it shut. They leave their marks in ways like these, before crossing the next threshold.

Confiscated Wings

The punishment was butterflies: staying at her desk and writing down everything she could find and remember from lessons about these dust-winged insects. Some have ears in their wings, she scribbled furiously, like Monarchs, not moths. Hollow veins that carry sound or a blood-like liquid that's cold and needs the sun to live. Wing tip to wing tip, an inch or two of fragile land. On the ground you might mistake them for leaves. Their coloured scales on our fingers are damaged flight or death. Chalk Hill Blue, Swallowtail, Peacock, Monarch, Red Admiral, Wood White and the Gatekeeper. Dwindling, endangered, extinct, rare. Staring at the rest of the paper he'd thumbed down in front of her, she recalled their overlapping voices exploding then fading down the corridor; sat up and looked through the window to where her class had fled the playground for the hill, parachuting the wind inside their jackets, towards the barricade of teachers below. That's how she was caught, laughing too much to see where she was going. It was the pigeons that got her—winging full-pelt towards the window, banging and sliding down the glass, toppling off the sill, expressionless and disappearing, another one close behind. She understands now why he chose butterflies: wings for flight and the freedom she'd miss on the hill, colours for wounds when crossing a glass line, and silence, for mocking and breaking apart the way it's meant to travel, defy boundaries and survive.

The Webbed Harlequin

Just two red spots into the world and already snared: thrashing wings and legs against a Spring breeze and the tacky glue of a highwire. Meanwhile, the spider is notable by its absence—onto other colours it hunts the opposite way with absolute trust in its fabric; so well versed in his pattern of life and death, spit one, hurl one, spit one, hurl.

Fruit Roulette

There is no traceable line or narrative from the apples of Eden and Snow White to the needles currently being found inside fruit. So, we continue to hunt the main antagonist; going after and narrowing down the evil Queens behind these cruel plots. Along the way we find Listeria in cantaloupes, Hepatitis A in pomegranates and needles in bananas. Silent, but deliberate as needles in strawberries. A delicate sleight of hand—if ever there was one—the quiet slide of metal inside such forgiving fruit, whose skin is already pin-pricked and closes behind itself. These gloved and slippered journeys set out to ransack life in a solitary bite. After the incidents and the headlines, we are told to be vigilant; to stay away and go about our lives as usual. But there is no usual for adults after Eden, for children after Snow White. No usual when death, disfigurement and bitterness are explained by a fruit that's passed through so many entrusted hands between soil and mouth, to stop randomly inside the absent heart of one.

The Circus Seat

Just as you sat upon your bicycle, the world threw you off: well,
not the world, but a warped version inside it. Certainly something
the system helped make; that blew ours apart and said—you can
shatter, die and never return.

Stage Four: Egg Overwintered

To Pocket a Star

She wants to find a way to hold snow in her mouth, pause its crystalized order on her tongue and know it well enough to recall when her limbs are in chaos. If she feeds her head this kind of magic, perhaps the body will follow.

Sylvie's River

She teaches us from scratch about what we think we've known and seen, said and done. Things we pick up, how they are named, titles they inherit—she tells us stories about them; gives everything from the rock to the wind-blown rose new labels. Take this carpet in the living room—it's not a carpet, it's a river-bed. And the river itself she makes from lights—red flashing ones for the fish, white for the ripples, the wire the water itself. She talks about *magic words* and asks me to tell her about them as she fishes from an orange bucket, *lying down up*. Her mouth is listening, watching where I direct a name, but her eye is restless, fidgeting over translation. As she talks, her hands dip left and right; she has a red plastic recorder for a rod, a green paper party hat wound about its tip, a feather-light loop wafts over a wooden fish. Suddenly, the world is less about trout and lexicons, than Eeyore, drooped on the other side of the riverbank. *Eeyore!* she declares, *needs a rescue!* As she leaps from her bucket, he tips forward into the water, his body going from grey to a slow play of red on, red off. *Poor Eeyore!* she cries, tearing the river away, casting it over the riverbank into the kitchen. Picked up, he goes back to grey again; out of danger, safely away from the pulse and blink of water, to warm and understood in her quick, no-nonsense hands.

The Paper Piano

Too broke to play the real thing, the boy gathered, cut and arranged eighty-eight pieces of scrap paper across a table. He drew black keys as they were meant to sit and define the white land in between; a stretched, flat place full of the promise of highs and lows. Then he watched others play on a screen; telescoped his gaze towards their dancing fingers and listened to the notes as they rose and fell under skilled steps; racing, pouncing, hovering and alighting across the ivory. After a while he'd memorised and heard enough to graduate from screen to paper, to the real thing, and back to paper again. When he'd mastered the cut-out version years later, he would sometimes make mistakes. *I made a mistake*, he would say, no longer a boy. *You can slip up on a torn piano*, he'd come out laughing; fall the wrong side of the white space, hit the bum notes. Today, he's trained to hear mistakes as music. Less the hopeless thud of soft-tipped bone on wood, with a cruel whisper of regret in return, than a sketch that sings off the table; fingers that catch and scale the wind, each time it fails to land in the same way.

The World on a Table

That lively note, turned sunny-side up, funded an evening of yellow and red symbols; songs in clicks, taps and sweeps, until caught and muffled in the hanging mouths of corner nets. They read their fate in rolling, shunted orbs as they win and lose over the soft green face of the table. Fixate on the little landscape, clock the changing ratio between the two main colours. Hit and miss these patterns, but at the lucky fluke-induced strikes they revive; reset each other with an acoustic kiss on the cheek.

Green

Once upon a time, green was a colour. Since then, a fitful way of living, a fragile approach, a tested, untested belief. Today, Green is politic, a trial, a bench in the House of Commons. A debated field, empty spaces in waiting, city greens temporarily colonised by a giant's wheel, fairground or circus; snatched squares of play, theory—the first time blue and yellow bleed into one another, labelled 'complementary' opposite purple on the colour wheel. We need to aim higher: place it back between a child's thumbs: watch to hear its instrumental breathing.

Little Ecocides

In the beginning, the garden kept its mouth shut: did not wince when its Dogwood was clipped and chucked in the workman's barrow; held its breath when the gardener gouged a pit into its knee, stuffed it with old papers, twigs and dried pine. But at flames stitched into its leg, and the last of its bloom wheeled towards the fire's restless sigh, the landscape opened its eyes—held them wide until the moon rose. During the day it made notes: clocked how tightly his gloves gripped the wheelbarrow's handles, how ungiving the hinge of his elbows, while the lost chatter of branches fell left and right of his chest. It highlighted the ways he refused to watch the sky while persuading smoke between the clouds—suffocated the blue and made a stranger of the sunlight. Underneath him, the grass bruises and bleeds as he digs down with his spade, his boots stamping out the dulled cry of metal, thud by thud. The ground spews out worms, ants, beetles, rooks, woodlice, butterflies and spiders—their confusion makes light and dark of the earth. When the gardener reaches the fire, tiptoed, he lifts the arms of his barrow and commits the earth to the flames. As he turns, quick as a wasp an ember catches his leg. Going back towards the house, he returns to the ground's head, cursing like a schoolboy and slapping his calf every second step—less of a man than this morning, he has one good hand to cover his ears from the charge of tongues behind him.

Blind Listening

They didn't time things well or listen ahead of the warnings—the protest-whispers of rushed saplings, mono-shopped into the ground, the shaking heads of jumbled birds and trees. The over-use of water; under-use of authorised touch. *It's not too late!* they clamour, for the final-placed *no more*—to make up for time, to get the leftover earth to where and how it needs to be.

Goodnight Yesterday

Time she put the past to bed. Gather it up carefully like a new-born, with a quick cry of recognition, if not of love. Then over the shoulder, up the stairs and down into the cradle. By morning, she vowed to hold it; start afresh, anew, again.

Best Before Tomorrow

Call time on oil, glitter, poison and waste; let fish sweep our coldblooded imprints from their ocean-beds. Commit to listening and tell the truth in set-texts. Before today closes, prescribe wild grass over Astro Turf, sea-life over trawlers, re-bake *bread in name only*. Witness, then act consciously before your next move towards litter or gold. Take note of the word care—its branding and meaning billowing everywhere and nowhere, like castles of wind on a burning moat. Rewild love; don't sell it.

Spade of Air

Hope is not terribly helpful at the moment she said, but admitting what we're doing and understanding the effect is: that after trashing someone else's and your own house repeatedly, it starts to have an impact on the rooms themselves, and the little ones inside them.

Airborne

March, and there's a fear brewing in the air and of the air itself. Windows stay closed and joggers are becoming reviled. Our hands have become the enemy of our faces and the language of war is infecting televised speeches, to keep us safe from sitting in public or falling in private. A medic takes time she doesn't have to alert us to where they are, and where we shall be, again. This is our core class. We are meant to take notes, but we don't. We wait. Have another cup of tea. Shake more hands or greet with a kiss: once, twice, three times back and forth bouncing from cheek to cheek: unchecked crime sweeping across unchecked mouths.

Grasshopper

We witnessed a hug on the street today. A man came out of his house, through his front garden and stopped by his gate, while someone crossed the road towards him; a clip at the back of his heel, smiling full beam ahead. Straight after—an awkward, but loving fury about it—they stepped back from each other, warmed to the brim then horrified. Calculating the length of an elephant, one retreated the prudent side of his blue wooden gate, while the other hovered on the edge of the kerb. Both commented on the narrowness of the pavement and the closing sky, then went their separate ways. Not long before, we'd been walking through the city's heart and although they say it dreams—the spires at least— today we caught it. Dreaming so soundly, looking so far from any kind of waking, you could hear a feather fall from a rook's landing, collide with the air that moved around a fuss of pigeons and settle on the road without fear of lifting. The Chapel, the House, the cafes and passages, all sleeping. Completely silent, were it not for one thing: the clock, the one they all come to see. No hands, just a giant mechanical body that keeps time once every five minutes; sends down the parade a deep echoing tick that falls from its own sound when striving to catch up. Rosalind the Grasshopper Clock, whose golden eyelids move so fast, you can miss the blink as you're watching.

Noli me Tangere

This was the year that the world was advised against touch. Not a country or two, not just every other handshake or the odd air kiss, but across the world, *noli me tangere* hovering in and out of legislation. Old language, new context was flown in, dictated from plastic podiums—phrases now stamped into chat on a virtual street corner: distancing, sanitise, shield, bubble, quarantine, isolate, lockdown. All these became the way of the hug, the lethal embrace. We continue to be advised against touch, but in the same breath told what we know: starvation is not good for the heart, mind, health and—stage-whispered—therefore, money. Behind the scenes some are inventing safe passages back over the tactile borders: cuddle curtains, hug-gloves, flexible corridors of plastic sleeves and cloaks. But this embrace will hurt. Choose carefully who comes first. Ask. Respect those who can't; never, rarely did. Plan your hugs. Wash before and after. Mask-up. Turn your face East to their West. Don't stay for long in there, no matter how your heart grows. Wash hands, change clothes. Mask-down. Think before you throw: which sea, which road, which living thing. Think about whether it was worth it. This is the year the hug faced extinction. Became a rare and shocking act to feel, see and know.

Eyes from the Wing

From a glider, he looks down at the virus; how it's cleared the streets, the roads, restaurants, parks, shops, schools, banks, youth centres, courts, commons, zoos, museums, venues, galleries, offices, centres, hotels. How it's filled hospitals, prisons; refilled hotels, colleges, churches, sometimes. And locked in forgotten spaces; trapped invisible faces. Someone moves onto an empty pavement, quiet, hunched, deep in thought, barely lifting his half-hidden head to another human walking in the other direction. From the sky, he can see they've forgotten how to speak, check, say hello. Our home is unmoored, coming away at the borders, while we're still trying to remember the right word for kindness.

The Blind Window

They share it—either side of the glass—this window love, this new way of thereness. They evolve; train their kiss and gestures to grow on mucky reflections. Mouth emphatically that they are doing OK and will come again tomorrow to this very spot, no matter how windy, how torrential, how earth-defyingly hot the air becomes. You from the sofa, the radiator, the carpet, the table and the box, will grow bigger, braver and taller, filling and towering past the frames, visit by visit. When we walk through each other's doors again and stay, we'll keep the glass as it is; a museum of silent repetitions, flower-pressed kisses of reassurance, a mosaic of bunched and open hands, a petri-dish of worries and un-flown wings. One day, we'll swap places; go the other way about the glass, to see what we look like inside-out, all blurry from years of never-ending smudges; an estranged species disorientated in space, being told to get ready to fly again.

Jane Monson lives in Cambridge as a poet, independent researcher and Specialist Mentor for disabled students at the University of Cambridge. Previously she was an Associate Lecturer in Creative Writing at Anglia Ruskin University. Her PhD is on the prose poetry of Francis Ponge and she has an MA in Creative Writing (poetry) from UEA. Jane is the editor of *This Line is not for Turning* (2011), an anthology of contemporary British prose poetry which Pascale Petit praised as 'groundbreaking' and more recently edited *British Prose Poetry: The Poems without Lines* (Palgrave Macmillan, 2018). She is widely anthologised in the UK and her prose poetry and reviews have been featured UK-wide and internationally in *Westerly, Fortnightly Review, Envoi, Aesthetica, Magma and Poetry London.* Jane's collections with Cinnamon include *Speaking Without Tongues* (2010) and *The Shared Surface* (2013). Cassandra Atherton, award-winning Australian prose poet and international expert and critic of the form has referred to Jane as 'the fairy godmother of prose poetry.'

Selected publications:

'One Foot; Many Places: The Prose Poem's Art of Standing Still While Travelling,' *Prose Poetry in Theory and Practice*, eds. Paul Hardwick and Anne Caldwell (forthcoming with Routledge).

The Prose Poem and the Anti-Novel: Unsettling Form in Nathalie Sarraute's *Tropismes*,' *EUP Companion to the Prose Poem*, eds., Michel Delville and Mary Ann Caws (Edinburgh, Edinburgh University Press, 2021).

'Six Poets; Many Voices,' Disability Feature, *Westerly Magazine*, (Crawley WA, Faculty of Arts, University of Western Australia, 2019).

'Square of Light: The Artist is Present,' in *The Valley Press Anthology of Prose Poetry*, eds., Anne Caldwell and Oz Hardwick (Calder Press, 2019).

World Poetry Day Podcast, Palgrave Macmillan, 2019: https://www.palgrave.com/gp/campaigns/world-poetry-day/jane-

Lightning Source UK Ltd.
Milton Keynes UK
UKHW041313240322
400560UK00012B/137